THE PLANNER + JOURNAL BELONGS TO

the Nudge

"BLESSED IS SHE WHO BELIEVED..."

LUKE 1:45

The Nudge Planner + Journal
Karri Turner, M.Div.

First Printing: July 2019
ISBN: 978-0-578-54260-7

All titles published by The Girl Bible, Inc., may be purchased in bulk for educational, business, fundraising or sales promotional use. For more information, please email info@thegirlbible.co.

THE **DEDICATION**

"For I know the plans I have for you," declares the Lord, "plans to prosper you and not to harm you, plans to give you hope and a future. Then you will call on me and come and pray to me, and I will listen to you. You will seek me and find me when you seek me with all your heart." - Jeremiah 29:11-13, New International Version (NIV)

Thank you Father for never swaying away from your plans for my life….. My inconsistency has never been an indicator of yours. I don't always comprehend your plans or your ways, but I am so grateful that you always understand and reveal what's best for me. I'm so grateful for your love and it being manifested daily as I walk the path that you've so beautifully laid out just for me. I will spend the rest of my life declaring your goodness and demonstrating the love and compassion that you have so recklessly shared with me, with others! Proud to be your daughter!

ACKNOWLEDGMENTS

To every person who just needs a Nudge, a powerful, stern, inspiring, motivating, loving push to help you move forward……. The Nudge Planner + Journal is just for you!

May it be just what you need at exactly the right time to give you the jolt needed to strategically activate your gifts at a higher level, finish what you started or bring into actualization the dreams that you have been harboring!

No greater time than NOW to become all you desired and more!

#ByHisGrace

I DO NOT APOLOGIZE FOR HOW I'M ABOUT TO MOVE.

Karri
KARRIANNA TURNER

FROM **KARRI'S** DESK

Hi! If you are taking a deep dive into this planner + journal, I can almost guarantee that there is something deep inside of you that wants more! You know that you have within you the ability to live higher, better and greater! However, you also know, that this new way of living is going to require a new level of focus and commitment from you! It's going to require the Nudge you need to get it done!

If you are ready to move into action instead of waiting for the perfect time to walk into your destiny, this amazing planner + journal is just for you! It's time to move from fantasy to fruition, from simply dreaming, to making your dreams your daily reality!

The Nudge Planner + Journal helps you stay accountable to your goals and includes personal nudges from me to help push and cheer you along the way. It's time to overcome the challenges and the excuses in your head and make your dreams a reality. This planner + journal includes monthly calendars and weekly breakdowns for you to track your progress. It also includes journal prompts and scriptures to keep the vision for your life in front of you. This is the planner + journal you'll be sure to carry around everywhere you go as you accomplish your goals like never before. My heart is to see you win! I desire to see you live the life that you've always desired! It's in you! The Nudge Planner + Journal is just the push you need to make it happen!!

I'm rooting for you!!

LOVE, **Karri**

BELIEVE IN YOUR COME UP.

KARRIANNA **TURNER**

WRITE A **LOVE LETTER**

It's time to dive into the next few months with focus and faith. Use the space below to write a love letter to yourself as a reminder of who God has created you to be. Come back to this letter when you need to encourage yourself.

_____

_____

_____

_____

_____

_____

_____

_____

_____

_____

MY Nudge CIRCLE

MY NUDGE CIRCLE

As you go through these months of working on your goals and dreams, don't forget about those who surround you as your friends, mentors, ect. Write their names down below and remember to pray for them daily.

NAME | _____

NAME | _____

NAME | _____

NAME | _____

NAME | _____

NAME | _____

NAME | _____

NAME | _____

NAME | _____

NAME | _____

NAME | _____

NAME | _____

A woman without a vision for her future will always return to her past.

Karri.
KARRIANNA TURNER

FOCUS ON **THE VISION**

Reading Time: Proverbs 29:18, Proverbs 16:3, Proverbs 21:5, Habakkuk 2:2-3, Philippians 3:14, Hebrews 10:35-36

Look up the definition for VISION and write it down below.

What is vision in your own words when you think about your own life?

Why is it important to have a vision for life?

No matter what we desire to do, we must always hear from God to truly know what and where we should go. Why is it important to hear God's voice to confirm our footsteps?

PRAYER TIME X **NUDGES FROM GOD**

Use the space below to write down things that God gives you in prayer.

_____

_____

_____

_____

_____

_____

_____

_____

_____

_____

_____

PRAYER TIME X **NUDGES FROM GOD**

Use the space below to write down things that God gives you in prayer.

_____

_____

_____

_____

_____

_____

_____

_____

_____

_____

_____

PRAYER TIME X **NUDGES FROM GOD**

Use the space below to write down things that God gives you in prayer.

_____

_____

_____

_____

_____

_____

_____

_____

_____

_____

PRAYER TIME X **NUDGES FROM GOD**

Use the space below to write down things that God gives you in prayer.

_____

_____

_____

_____

_____

_____

_____

_____

_____

_____

THIS MONTH_____ YEAR_____

SUN	MON	TUES	WED	THUR	FRI	SAT

NOTES: _____

_____

_____

SUNDAY

MONDAY

TUESDAY

WEDNESDAY

THURSDAY

FRIDAY

SATURDAY

IMPORTANT REMINDERS

NOTES FOR **THE WEEK**

_____

_____

_____

_____

_____

_____

_____

_____

_____

_____

_____

SUNDAY

MONDAY

TUESDAY

WEDNESDAY

THURSDAY

FRIDAY

SATURDAY

IMPORTANT REMINDERS

NOTES FOR **THE WEEK**

SUNDAY

MONDAY

TUESDAY

WEDNESDAY

THURSDAY

FRIDAY

SATURDAY

IMPORTANT REMINDERS

NOTES FOR **THE WEEK**

SUNDAY

MONDAY

TUESDAY

WEDNESDAY

THURSDAY

FRIDAY

SATURDAY

IMPORTANT REMINDERS

NOTES FOR **THE WEEK**

SUNDAY

MONDAY

TUESDAY

WEDNESDAY

THURSDAY

FRIDAY

SATURDAY

IMPORTANT REMINDERS

NOTES FOR **THE WEEK**

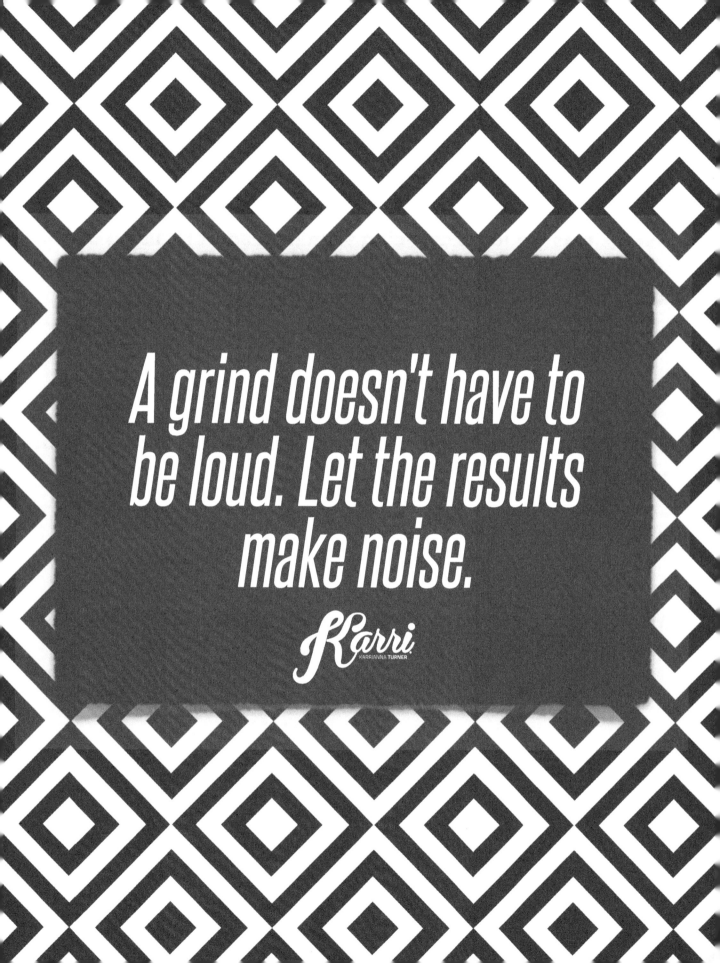

A grind doesn't have to be loud. Let the results make noise.

Karri
KARRIANNA TURNER

GRIND **FOR RESULTS**

Reading Time: Psalm 127:1-2, Proverbs 10:4-5, Proverbs 14:23-24, John 5:16, Colossians 3:17

Many times we focus on being seen instead of focusing on the work we must do. Have you ever been distracted by the announcements of others? What happened?

How will you focus more on the results than being loud about your ground this month?

What are some things you need to accomplish this month that require for you to be "below the radar"?

PRAYER TIME X **NUDGES FROM GOD**

Use the space below to write down things that God gives you in prayer.

_____

_____

_____

_____

_____

_____

_____

_____

_____

_____

PRAYER TIME X **NUDGES FROM GOD**

Use the space below to write down things that God gives you in prayer.

_____

_____

_____

_____

_____

_____

_____

_____

_____

_____

_____

PRAYER TIME X **NUDGES FROM GOD**

Use the space below to write down things that God gives you in prayer.

_____

_____

_____

_____

_____

_____

_____

_____

_____

_____

PRAYER TIME X **NUDGES FROM GOD**

Use the space below to write down things that God gives you in prayer.

_____

_____

_____

_____

_____

_____

_____

_____

_____

THIS MONTH_____ YEAR_____

SUN	MON	TUES	WED	THUR	FRI	SAT

NOTES: _____

_____

_____

SUNDAY

MONDAY

TUESDAY

WEDNESDAY

THURSDAY

FRIDAY

SATURDAY

IMPORTANT REMINDERS

NOTES FOR **THE WEEK**

SUNDAY

MONDAY

TUESDAY

WEDNESDAY

THURSDAY

FRIDAY

SATURDAY

IMPORTANT REMINDERS

NOTES FOR **THE WEEK**

_____

_____

_____

_____

_____

_____

_____

_____

_____

_____

_____

SUNDAY

MONDAY

TUESDAY

WEDNESDAY

THURSDAY

FRIDAY

SATURDAY

IMPORTANT REMINDERS

NOTES FOR **THE WEEK**

SUNDAY

MONDAY

TUESDAY

WEDNESDAY

THURSDAY

FRIDAY

SATURDAY

IMPORTANT REMINDERS

NOTES FOR **THE WEEK**

_____

_____

_____

_____

_____

_____

_____

_____

_____

_____

_____

SUNDAY

MONDAY

TUESDAY

WEDNESDAY

THURSDAY

FRIDAY

SATURDAY

IMPORTANT REMINDERS

NOTES FOR **THE WEEK**

BE **SECURE + CONFIDENT**

Reading Time: Psalm 84:11,Isaiah 40:29-31, Isaiah 43:2, Jeremiah 29:11, Deuteronomy 31:8,Romans 8:37-39, 2 Peter 1:4

When you're focused on your goals and accomplishing things in life, you can't allow the lies to blur the promise that God gave you. What are the lies that you need to cancel out in your head that are the opposite of God's promises to you?

Write down 10 "I AM" confessions stating who God has made you to be.
1. I AM _____.
2. I AM _____.
3. I AM _____.
4. I AM _____.
5. I AM _____.
6. I AM _____.
7. I AM _____.
8. I AM _____.
9. I AM _____.
10.I AM _____.

PRAYER TIME X **NUDGES FROM GOD**

Use the space below to write down things that God gives you in prayer.

_____

_____

_____

_____

_____

_____

_____

_____

_____

_____

PRAYER TIME X **NUDGES FROM GOD**

Use the space below to write down things that God gives you in prayer.

_____

_____

_____

_____

_____

_____

_____

_____

_____

_____

PRAYER TIME X **NUDGES FROM GOD**

Use the space below to write down things that God gives you in prayer.

_____

_____

_____

_____

_____

_____

_____

_____

_____

_____

PRAYER TIME X **NUDGES FROM GOD**

Use the space below to write down things that God gives you in prayer.

_____

_____

_____

_____

_____

_____

_____

_____

_____

_____

THIS MONTH_____ YEAR_____

SUN	MON	TUES	WED	THUR	FRI	SAT

NOTES: _____

_____

_____

SUNDAY

MONDAY

TUESDAY

WEDNESDAY

THURSDAY

FRIDAY

SATURDAY

IMPORTANT REMINDERS

NOTES FOR **THE WEEK**

SUNDAY

MONDAY

TUESDAY

WEDNESDAY

THURSDAY

FRIDAY

SATURDAY

IMPORTANT REMINDERS

NOTES FOR **THE WEEK**

_____

_____

_____

_____

_____

_____

_____

_____

_____

_____

SUNDAY

MONDAY

TUESDAY

WEDNESDAY

THURSDAY

FRIDAY

SATURDAY

IMPORTANT REMINDERS

NOTES FOR **THE WEEK**

SUNDAY

MONDAY

TUESDAY

WEDNESDAY

THURSDAY

FRIDAY

SATURDAY

IMPORTANT REMINDERS

NOTES FOR **THE WEEK**

SUNDAY

MONDAY

TUESDAY

WEDNESDAY

THURSDAY

FRIDAY

SATURDAY

IMPORTANT REMINDERS

NOTES FOR **THE WEEK**

_____

_____

_____

_____

_____

_____

_____

_____

_____

_____

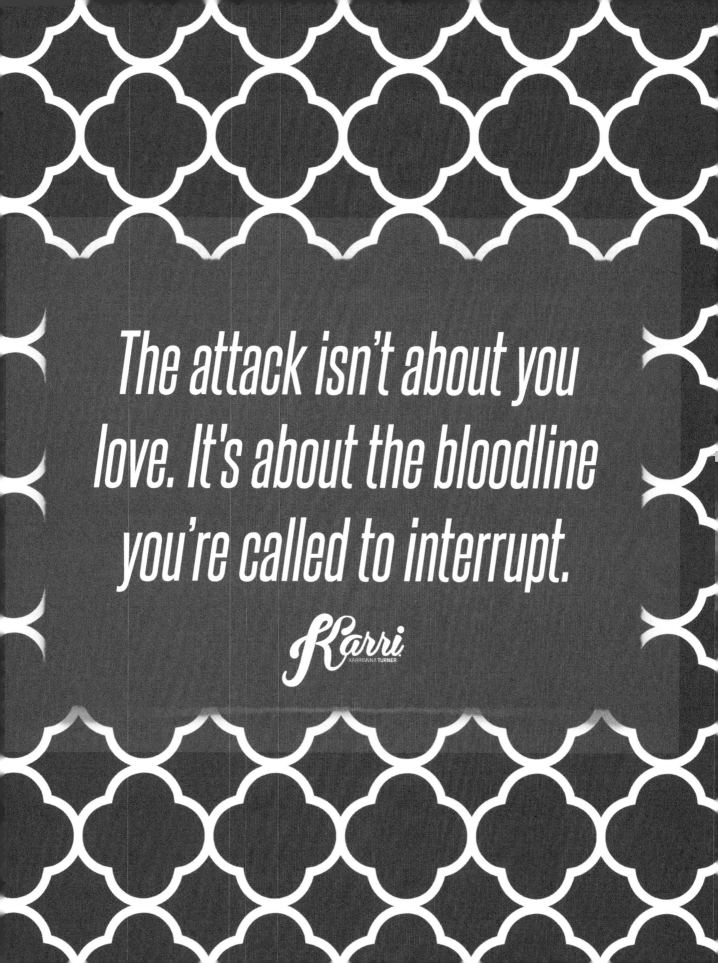

PREPARE **FOR ATTACK**

Reading Time: Isaiah 54:17, Luke 10:19, 1 John 4:4, 2 Corinthians 10:3-5, Ephesians 6:11-17, John 16:33, 1 Timothy 6:12

Perspective is everything when you're in a battle. It's not just seeing the battle but it's focusing on the victory in the midst of opposition. How will you equip yourself this month to face your battles?

You've been called to knock down barriers in your bloodline and unleash an anointed legacy through your life. Why do you believe the enemy comes after those who knock down barriers and mountains?

PRAYER TIME X **NUDGES FROM GOD**

Use the space below to write down things that God gives you in prayer.

_____

_____

_____

_____

_____

_____

_____

_____

_____

_____

PRAYER TIME X **NUDGES FROM GOD**

Use the space below to write down things that God gives you in prayer.

_____

_____

_____

_____

_____

_____

_____

_____

_____

_____

PRAYER TIME X **NUDGES FROM GOD**

Use the space below to write down things that God gives you in prayer.

_____

_____

_____

_____

_____

_____

_____

_____

_____

_____

PRAYER TIME X **NUDGES FROM GOD**

Use the space below to write down things that God gives you in prayer.

_____

_____

_____

_____

_____

_____

_____

_____

_____

_____

THIS MONTH_____ YEAR_____

SUN	MON	TUES	WED	THUR	FRI	SAT

NOTES: _____

_____

_____

SUNDAY

MONDAY

TUESDAY

WEDNESDAY

THURSDAY

FRIDAY

SATURDAY

IMPORTANT REMINDERS

NOTES FOR **THE WEEK**

SUNDAY

MONDAY

TUESDAY

WEDNESDAY

THURSDAY

FRIDAY

SATURDAY

IMPORTANT REMINDERS

NOTES FOR **THE WEEK**

SUNDAY

MONDAY

TUESDAY

WEDNESDAY

THURSDAY

FRIDAY

SATURDAY

IMPORTANT REMINDERS

NOTES FOR **THE WEEK**

_____

_____

_____

_____

_____

_____

_____

_____

_____

_____

SUNDAY

MONDAY

TUESDAY

WEDNESDAY

THURSDAY

FRIDAY

SATURDAY

IMPORTANT REMINDERS

NOTES FOR **THE WEEK**

_____

_____

_____

_____

_____

_____

_____

_____

_____

_____

SUNDAY

MONDAY

TUESDAY

WEDNESDAY

THURSDAY

FRIDAY

SATURDAY

IMPORTANT REMINDERS

NOTES FOR **THE WEEK**

A HEALTHY **HEART**

Reading Time: 2 Corinthians 5:17, Ezekiel 36:25-27, Psalm 51:10, Mark 7:21-23, Proverbs 4:23, Jeremiah 24:7, Matthew 6:1-4, Matthew 5:8

We have to protect our hearts as we grow and make moves in life. What are some things you need to remove from your heart?

When was the last time you compared your life to another? How does comparison and jealously distract us from our destiny?

How do we keep our hearts pure before God?

PRAYER TIME X **NUDGES FROM GOD**

Use the space below to write down things that God gives you in prayer.

_____

_____

_____

_____

_____

_____

_____

_____

_____

_____

PRAYER TIME X **NUDGES FROM GOD**

Use the space below to write down things that God gives you in prayer.

_____

_____

_____

_____

_____

_____

_____

_____

_____

_____

PRAYER TIME X **NUDGES FROM GOD**

Use the space below to write down things that God gives you in prayer.

_____

_____

_____

_____

_____

_____

_____

_____

_____

_____

PRAYER TIME X **NUDGES FROM GOD**

Use the space below to write down things that God gives you in prayer.

_____

_____

_____

_____

_____

_____

_____

_____

_____

_____

THIS MONTH_____ YEAR_____

SUN	MON	TUES	WED	THUR	FRI	SAT

NOTES: _____

_____

_____

SUNDAY

MONDAY

TUESDAY

WEDNESDAY

THURSDAY

FRIDAY

SATURDAY

IMPORTANT REMINDERS

NOTES FOR **THE WEEK**

SUNDAY

MONDAY

TUESDAY

WEDNESDAY

THURSDAY

FRIDAY

SATURDAY

IMPORTANT REMINDERS

NOTES FOR **THE WEEK**

SUNDAY

MONDAY

TUESDAY

WEDNESDAY

THURSDAY

FRIDAY

SATURDAY

IMPORTANT REMINDERS

NOTES FOR **THE WEEK**

_____

_____

_____

_____

_____

_____

_____

_____

_____

_____

SUNDAY

MONDAY

TUESDAY

WEDNESDAY

THURSDAY

FRIDAY

SATURDAY

IMPORTANT REMINDERS

NOTES FOR **THE WEEK**

SUNDAY

MONDAY

TUESDAY

WEDNESDAY

THURSDAY

FRIDAY

SATURDAY

IMPORTANT REMINDERS

NOTES FOR **THE WEEK**

DECLARE **YOUR OVERFLOW**

Reading Time: Psalm 5:12, Psalm 90:17, Psalm 84:11, Ephesians 1:3, 2 Corinthians 9:8, Numbers 6:24-26, Psalm 31:19, Psalm 23:6, Revelation 3:7, Jeremiah 17:7-8

Favor truly isn't favor. Favor also isn't accidental. Favor is on purpose and intentional because it's a shadow that follows you as a child of God. Write down your own favor confession for this month that you'll declare daily.

You can't expect something that you aren't preparing for. How are you making room for the blessings and favor that is coming your way?

PRAYER TIME X **NUDGES FROM GOD**

Use the space below to write down things that God gives you in prayer.

_____

_____

_____

_____

_____

_____

_____

_____

_____

_____

_____

PRAYER TIME X **NUDGES FROM GOD**

Use the space below to write down things that God gives you in prayer.

_____

_____

_____

_____

_____

_____

_____

_____

_____

_____

PRAYER TIME X **NUDGES FROM GOD**

Use the space below to write down things that God gives you in prayer.

_____

_____

_____

_____

_____

_____

_____

_____

_____

_____

_____

PRAYER TIME X **NUDGES FROM GOD**

Use the space below to write down things that God gives you in prayer.

_____

_____

_____

_____

_____

_____

_____

_____

_____

_____

THIS MONTH_____ YEAR_____

SUN	MON	TUES	WED	THUR	FRI	SAT

NOTES: _____

_____

_____

SUNDAY

MONDAY

TUESDAY

WEDNESDAY

THURSDAY

FRIDAY

SATURDAY

IMPORTANT REMINDERS

NOTES FOR **THE WEEK**

SUNDAY

MONDAY

TUESDAY

WEDNESDAY

THURSDAY

FRIDAY

SATURDAY

IMPORTANT REMINDERS

NOTES FOR **THE WEEK**

SUNDAY

MONDAY

TUESDAY

WEDNESDAY

THURSDAY

FRIDAY

SATURDAY

IMPORTANT REMINDERS

NOTES FOR **THE WEEK**

SUNDAY

MONDAY

TUESDAY

WEDNESDAY

THURSDAY

FRIDAY

SATURDAY

IMPORTANT REMINDERS

NOTES FOR **THE WEEK**

_____

_____

_____

_____

_____

_____

_____

_____

_____

_____

_____

SUNDAY

MONDAY

TUESDAY

WEDNESDAY

THURSDAY

FRIDAY

SATURDAY

IMPORTANT REMINDERS

NOTES FOR **THE WEEK**

GO FORTH.

Karri
KARRIANNA TURNER

ABOUT THE AUTHOR

Karri Turner, M.Div., a native of Las Vegas, Nevada is one of the nations' most vibrant, promising and emerging leaders. Karri wears many hats as a CEO, Author, Speaker, Entrepreneur and Philanthropist.

Karri Turner has received numerous awards and honors such as being named Who's Who Among American Colleges and Universities, the Distinguished Leadership and Service Award from the City of Atlanta, and The Valor Award for Outstanding Leadership & Service. She was selected as a Fellow in the prestigious Front Line Leaders Academy, where she was elected the People For the American Way Foundation, Youth Ambassador.

She is also an alumna of the Atlanta Women's Foundation, Destiny Fund, and former participant of the White House Project's, New York City, Go Run Training. Karri is an alumna of the United Way (V.I.P.) Volunteer Involvement Program and member of Alpha Kappa Alpha Sorority, Incorporated, former Basileus of Gamma Gamma Chapter.

In a world in search of new leadership, Karri Turner is at the forefront of a new generation of exceptional leaders. Karri holds a Bachelor of Arts degree in Political Science from the legendary Morris Brown College and a Master of Divinity Degree from The Candler School of Theology at Emory University. Karri is currently pursuing a Doctorate in Ministry with a concentration in Christian Leadership & Renewal. Karri is the published author of "The Girl Bible" and "She's Lit." Karri is an ordained clergywoman and motivational speaker who travels the country inspiring women!

Let's Stay in Touch!

@MZKARRIBABY

KARRI TURNER, M.DIV.

@THEKARRITURNER

KARRITURNER.ORG

KARRI'S FAVORITE BOOKS

THE GIRL BIBLE
SHE'S LIT

Shop Online | www.karriturner.org
Also available on Amazon

KARRITURNER.ORG

Made in the USA
Middletown, DE
07 July 2025

10202283R00084